SUPER-AWESOME SCIENCE

THE SCIENCE OF WARRIORS

by Cecilia Pinto McCarthy

Content Consultant
Wayne E. Lee, PhD
Professor of History
University of North Carolina at Chapel Hill

Core Library

An Imprint of Abdo Publishing
abdopublishing.com

abdopublishing.com

Published by Abdo Publishing, a division of ABDO, PO Box 398166, Minneapolis, Minnesota 55439. Copyright © 2017 by Abdo Consulting Group, Inc. International copyrights reserved in all countries. No part of this book may be reproduced in any form without written permission from the publisher. Core Library™ is a trademark and logo of Abdo Publishing.

Printed in the United States of America, North Mankato, Minnesota
042016
092016

Cover Photo: Shutterstock Images
Interior Photos: Shutterstock Images, 1, 22; North Wind Picture Archives, 4, 36; Marc Dufresne/iStockphoto, 6; Classic Image/Alamy, 10; Terry W. Rutledge/National Geographic, 13; Alice Day/Shutterstock Images, 15; Kimimasa Mayama/EPA/Newscom, 17, 45; Daily Mirror Mirrorpix/Newscom, 19; Jonathan Blair/Corbis, 25; Przemek Tokar/Shutterstock Images, 27, 43; Spc. David Barnes/US Army, 30; Album/Prisma/Newscom, 32; Artwork Studio BKK/Shutterstock Images, 34; Mass Communication Specialist Seaman Zachary S. Welch/US Navy, 38

Editor: Jon Westmark
Series Designer: Jake Nordby

Publisher's Cataloging in Publication Data
Names: McCarthy, Cecilia Pinto, author.
Title: The science of warriors / by Cecilia Pinto McCarthy.
Description: Minneapolis, MN : Abdo Publishing, [2017] | Series: Super-awesome
    science | Includes bibliographical references and index.
Identifiers: LCCN 2015960590 | ISBN 9781680782530 (lib. bdg.) |
    ISBN 9781680776645 (ebook)
Subjects: LCSH: Soldiers--Juvenile literature.
Classification: DDC 355--dc23
LC record available at http://lccn.loc.gov/2015960590

CONTENTS

CHAPTER ONE

GAINING AN EDGE

The Greek hoplite warriors stand ready to move into battle. They overlap their bronze-covered shields, forming a wall. Their armor is made of layered fabric thick enough to deflect enemy attacks. Each hoplite grips a spear eight feet (2.4 m) long. The spear's central ridge makes the tip stronger. At their sides, each hoplite carries a double-edged sword. Its well-balanced blade makes it easy to swing.

Greek hoplites used a tight formation called a phalanx to shield one another.

Improvements in iron and steel helped change the way warriors battled.

Through the Ages

From prehistoric fighters to modern-day soldiers, science and technology have improved warriors' chances on the battlefield. With science behind them, warriors have protected their homelands and conquered new territories.

The earliest conflicts involved hand-to-hand combat. In time workers learned to mold metals. People forged strong clubs and swords of bronze, iron, and steel. With more powerful weapons came the need for better protection. Metal armor was created and used along with leather and fabric armor.

Harnessing the power of machines made weapons even more powerful. Projectiles shot from machines were more effective than those thrown by hand. The invention of gunpowder ushered in a new era of projectiles—and warfare. Cannons and guns were born.

Technology also revolutionized military transportation. The chariot gave Egyptian soldiers an advantage on land. Superior shipbuilding allowed Vikings to travel to and take faraway lands. The invention of the combustion engine, the steam engine, and nuclear energy each changed how militaries moved.

IN THE REAL WORLD
The Cold War

Nations sometimes compete with each other to develop the best weapons in what is called an arms race. After World War II (1939–1945), the United States and the Soviet Union struggled with each other to become the top superpower. This time of competition was called the Cold War (1947–1991). The war did not involve soldiers fighting. Instead each country spent billions of dollars building its military to try to get ahead of the other.

Animals in War

Not all war tactics involve new technologies. Animal behavior experts sometimes train animals to perform wartime tasks. During World War I (1914–1918), soldiers attached messages to pigeons' legs. The birds instinctively flew to their coops, where other soldiers received the messages. Dogs, dolphins, and seals have also been wartime helpers. Dogs can sniff out hidden explosives. Dolphins and seals can find underwater mines and retrieve objects. Other animals do not need training. Slugs naturally shrink when they detect poisonous gas. During World War I, soldiers brought slugs into battle. When the slugs scrunched up, the soldiers knew to put on their gas masks.

Modern Military

Science is still driving improvements in the military. Chemists develop new armor materials to keep soldiers safe. Physicists and engineers design more effective weapons and combat vehicles. Computer technology flies military planes and directs missiles. Drones and robots take over dangerous tasks. Some scientific advancements meant for military purposes have become part of everyday life.

Robert A. Millikan was a physicist who won the Nobel Prize in 1923. After World War I, he wrote about the connection between war and science. Below is an excerpt from that article:

> *But what have all these accomplishments of science in the war to do with the new opportunity in science? Simply this; for the first time in history the world has been waked up by the war to an appreciation of what science can do. Why have we gone on for hundreds of years wasting millions and hundreds of millions of dollars in collisions between ships? Why have we not years ago in times of peace gone at the problems of under-water detection in the way in which we went at them during the war? Simply because men in authority have been asleep to the possibilities. But now . . . they are awake. . . . But just now the war has taught our political and industrial leaders what science can do. The war has also taught young soldiers that they need their science for success.*
>
> Source: Robert A. Millikan. "A New Opportunity in Science." Science 50.1291 (1919): 292. Print.

Back It Up

In this passage, Millikan uses evidence to support a point. Write a paragraph describing his main point and the evidence he uses to support that point.

WINNING WEAPONS

Early peoples hunted animals and gathered food from plants. They used rocks to make sharp spearheads and axes out of flint. They made spears from long sticks hardened in fire. In approximately 8000 BCE, people began to settle in larger communities. They formed armies to protect themselves and their lands. To be successful in battle, civilizations needed to develop the best weapons.

Sargon of Akkad formed the world's first empire in approximately 2300 BCE.

Body Force

The first weapons were handheld. A club is the simplest type of hand weapon. Its effectiveness depends on its weight and how fast it is swung. Adding weight onto the striking end of the club increases its momentum. Momentum is the mass of an object multiplied by its velocity. More momentum means a club will do more damage when it hits.

Warriors around the world used clubs. Native Americans attacked with clubs fitted with spikes and stones. Warriors of the South Pacific bashed enemies with clubs studded with razor-sharp sharks' teeth.

Metallurgy launched a new age of improved handheld weapons. Metallurgy is the science of metals. People learned that fire could melt and shape metal. They could make swords with sharp edges. The first metal used was copper. It was plentiful and easy to work with. But copper weapons were weak. They could not hold up to the forces of battle.

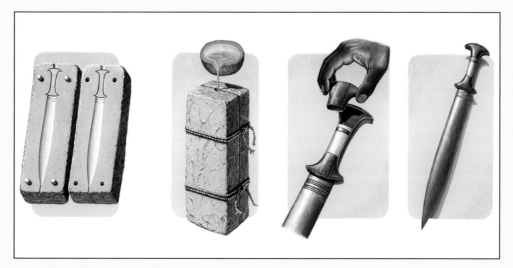

Bronze Age Swords

Swords made of bronze were cast. To cast a sword, liquid metal is poured into a mold using a ladle. The mold is in the shape of the sword. After the metal cools, pieces of the handle are added so the sword can be gripped more easily. From what you have read, what makes bronze a good metal to cast?

In approximately 3000 BCE, metalworkers accidentally created a new metal called bronze. Bronze is an alloy, or mixture, of copper and tin. Bronze melts at a lower temperature than copper does, making it easier to work with. Bronze made hard, long-lasting weapons that kept a sharp edge. Before bronze, metalworkers could only make short-bladed daggers. But bronze was strong enough to be made into longer blades.

The Broadsword

Knights of the Middle Ages took down their opponents with a variety of metal weapons. One common weapon was the broadsword made of iron or steel. The broadsword had a wide blade and two cutting edges. A groove called a fuller ran the length of the blade. The fuller lightened the weight of the sword without reducing its strength. The sword's point of balance, or center of mass, was an important design feature. The center of mass is the place at which the sword's weight is concentrated. When the sword is held at this point, it balances. A properly balanced sword can be more easily handled. If a sword's weight is too far toward the tip, it will be difficult to lift and swing.

In approximately 1200 BCE, metalsmiths started using iron instead of bronze. Blades made of iron were stronger and could be forged into long, heavy swords. While working with iron, smiths discovered that a new metal was formed when charcoal from the forging fire mixed with iron. This new metal was steel. Steel was harder than bronze and iron. Steel blades were tough. Their edges stayed sharp. Iron and steel were used for thousands of years.

Flails were effective in avoiding the enemies' shields.
But they were more difficult to use for defense.

During the Middle Ages, iron and steel swords, clubs, and flails were popular weapons. Maces are a type of club. The hard head of a mace usually did not pierce armor. But a powerful blow from a mace could break bones. A flail is a club fitted with a spiked ball attached to the end of a chain. The chain adds velocity to the ball. More velocity means more momentum. Knights swinging flails could reach over their opponents' shields. Flails delivered powerful blows to the heads of enemies.

Projectiles

The development of projectile weapons was an important milestone in war technology. Using a projectile allowed warriors to attack from a distance. Projectiles could be launched or thrown at the enemy. Two forces affect the trajectory, or flight path, of all projectiles: gravity and air resistance. As a projectile moves toward its target, the force of gravity pulls it toward Earth. Meanwhile air resistance, or drag, pushes in the opposite direction of the projectile.

Ancient bows and arrows were projectile weapons that date back at least 12,000 years. Bows work by transferring the energy provided by the archer to the arrow. As the arrow is pulled back on a drawstring, the flexible bow bends. This stored energy is called potential energy. When the arrow is released, potential energy becomes kinetic energy. Kinetic energy is the energy of motion. An arrow pulled back as far as possible will have greater kinetic energy. It travels faster and farther.

Starting in the 1100s CE, Japanese samurai warriors competed in *yabusame*, a mounted archery competition, to prepare for battle. The sport is still practiced today.

Arrows do not fly straight on their own. They bend around the bow when shot. Arrows flex back and forth as they fly. Adding vanes, or fins, to the tail ends of arrows makes them spin. Spinning arrows become more stable and fly straight.

The trebuchet is another projectile weapon. The trebuchet was invented in China in approximately 300 BCE. The weapon consists of a long beam that pivots on a frame. A sling attaches to one end of the beam. It holds a payload of rock. In early trebuchets, people pulled down on the opposite end of the beam, launching the rock. Later forms used heavy objects called counterweights. In these machines, the payload end of the beam gets pulled down. This lifts the counterweight. When the payload end releases, gravity pulls the counterweight down. The counterweight's potential energy turns to kinetic energy. The energy sends the payload airborne.

Explosives

Projectile weapons became more effective and deadly after the invention of gunpowder. Gunpowder, first called black powder, used the force of a chemical explosion to propel projectiles.

Gunpowder originated in China in the 800s BCE. Monks mixing ingredients for medicine accidentally made gunpowder. The monks were using saltpeter, a natural compound. Setting fire to a mixture of saltpeter, sulfur, and carbon caused a reaction. The reaction released hot, expanding gases. Eventually, the expanding gas was used to power projectiles.

As technology improved, cannons changed the way naval battles were fought.

Gunpowder eventually led to the development of cannons in China in the 1100s. The simplest cannons were metal tubes that fired heavy stones or iron balls. Cannons evolved into more accurate weapons with devastating power. Their explosive blasts crushed castle walls.

Another weapon resulting from gunpowder was the gun. Originally guns were small versions of cannons that shot small cannonballs. Modern guns shoot bullets. Bullet cartridges contain both the bullet and the gunpowder. When the gun's trigger is pulled, the firing pin hits the cartridge, igniting a small charge, called a primer. The charge then explodes, creating gases that expand. These gases in turn force the bullet out of its case and out of the barrel of the gun.

New Developments

Today people use more advanced projectile weapons. Missiles are one type of modern projectile. Many missiles have systems that steer them toward their targets. Some missiles, such as the portable Stinger, are launched by soldiers toward targets. Stingers track heat and steer themselves. Other missiles use radar to find their targets. Radar uses radio waves to find objects. A radar detector sends out signals then waits for the waves to bounce off of nearby objects.

Many factors ensure a missile hits its target. Scientists determine the correct amount of fuel and explosives a missile must carry to be effective. How far and fast a missile travels can be influenced by wind and air temperature. Soldiers use computers to check wind speed and direction, air temperature, and air density. They adjust the missile's trajectory as needed.

EXPLORE ONLINE

Chapter Two describes the invention of gunpowder. The website below features a brief history of gunpowder. How is the information from the website similar to the information in Chapter Two? What new information did you learn from the website?

How Gunpowder Changed the World

mycorelibrary.com/science-of-warriors

PROTECTION TECHNOLOGY

People have protected themselves with armor for thousands of years. Weapons can injure a warrior in two ways. The force of a weapon can damage the body by only hitting it, or a weapon can harm a body by piercing it. A weapon hits a warrior's body with a force. Armor protects by pushing back against the force of the weapon. If the weapon's force is greater than the armor's, it will pierce the armor.

Plate armor was used to protect against slashing sword blows.

Ancient people made armor from animal skins and bones tied together with cords. As groups of people began to fight one another with more advanced weapons, armor needed to offer more protection.

Ancient Greek warriors went into battle wearing both soft armor and bronze-plated armor. The soft armor was called *linothorax*. It was made of layers of linen glued together. Having layers helped spread out the force of a weapon's impact. It gave linothorax increased shear strength. A material's shear strength measures how much stress it can take before it breaks.

Mail and Plate Armor

Iron and steel were not only turned into deadly weapons. These metals also were shaped into helmets, body plates, and shields. Warriors in Europe and Asia used a metal armor called chain mail for hundreds of years. Mail is made from thousands of interlocking metal rings. The best mail suits were made from iron links riveted in a tight overlapping

Knights in the Middle Ages protected their horses with plate armor and chain mail.

pattern. Mail was flexible enough to be fitted to a warrior's body. Warriors covered their heads, torsos, and legs with mail. Tightly woven mail armor provided protection from slashing swords. But it did little to protect the wearer from heavy blows.

Plate armor offered more protection than mail from bows and early guns. Medieval knights covered themselves from head to toe with plate armor. To make plate armor, large pieces of iron were heated in a fire. Metalworkers sometimes changed the iron into hard steel by adding carbon from the charcoal in the fire. The metal was then hammered into shape and polished. Hard plate armor was effective because it was difficult to cut through. It led to a rise in blunt-force weapons.

Hiding in Plain Sight

Another way warriors protect themselves from harm is by disguising themselves. The use of disguise for military purposes has been around for hundreds of years. The practice became more common as long-range rifles entered use. By World War I, the French military created a department devoted to camouflage, or clothing that blends in with its surroundings.

Ghillie suits use leaves, twigs, and grass to allow soldiers to blend in with certain environments.

The two most important elements of camouflage clothing are color and pattern. Camouflage is made in dull shades that match the colors of areas where soldiers fight. The greens, browns, whites, and grays mimic the colors of plants, soils, sand, snow, or buildings. Camouflage works because the human brain tends to group similar colors together as units. The brain does not perceive blotchy patches of color

Liquid Armor

An ongoing issue with body armor is how to make it both effective and comfortable to wear. One solution is to use a special fluid with tiny silica particles. Silica is found in sand. The particles float in the liquid. As they float, the particles repel one another. When something hits the fluid, the impact energy overcomes the forces keeping the particles apart. The particles are instead drawn to one other. They form solid clumps. Vests soaked in this fluid do not need as many layers of Kevlar. The fluid does not change the flexibility of Kevlar. But it does change its strength. Kevlar treated with the liquid does not stretch as far when hit. This keeps projectiles from getting close to the soldier's body.

on camouflage clothing as separate objects. The patterns break up the overall shape of the soldier's body, blending it with the surroundings.

Kevlar

Many modern soldiers wear both camouflage and a form of armor. Today's soldiers wear armor made from synthetic, or man-made, fibers. The fibers are made from polymers. Polymers contain long chains of repeated molecules. The type of molecules and the way they are arranged gives a polymer its particular properties. Kevlar is a type of plastic made from polymer. The material is spun into fibers that are then woven into Kevlar mats.

Kevlar's most important quality is its strength. Kevlar is five times stronger than steel. The layers of material in a Kevlar vest can deform the tip of a speeding bullet. When a bullet hits Kevlar, the material spreads out the force of the impact. This prevents serious injury. Soldiers can insert metal or ceramic plates in special pockets for added protection.

FURTHER EVIDENCE

Chapter Three has quite a bit of information about the use of armor throughout history. What was one of the main points of the chapter? What evidence did the author give to support this point? Go to the article about medieval armor at the website below. Does the information on the website support the main point of the chapter? What new evidence does it present?

The History of Medieval Armor

mycorelibrary.com/science-of-warriors

CHAPTER FOUR

VEHICLES OF VICTORY

part from having superior weapons and armor, using the best vehicles also gives warriors an advantage in battle. Some vehicles transport warriors effectively. Other vehicles have weapons that give the soldiers an edge. Still others provide protection or a base of operation. As warfare has moved from land to sea to sky, having the best transportation has often chosen the winner in battle.

Mine-resistant ambush protected (MRAP) vehicles are designed to safely transport soldiers.

Egyptian chariots often carried a driver and a warrior.

Conquering Land

The Egyptian horse-drawn chariots of more than 3,000 years ago were marvels of engineering. They gave warriors the advantage on flat land. The chariot consisted of a floor frame and a pole that fit into an axle. The socket where the two parts joined was left loose, so that the pole could move in and out freely.

The looseness allowed the floor frame to move and act like a shock absorber.

The Egyptians used animal fat to lubricate wheel parts. The slippery fat reduced friction caused by rubbing parts. Reduced friction meant the chariots could travel faster and for longer periods. The chariot's axle and wheels were positioned toward the back of the vehicle. This prevented the rider from standing on the axle, making for a smoother ride. The Egyptians experimented with the number of wheel spokes to improve the chariot's speed. They made chariots with four, six, and eight spokes. The more spokes, the more rigid and supportive the wheel. They settled on a six-spoke design. It gave the chariot strength without slowing it down.

War Engine

The invention of the internal combustion engine in the late 1800s began a new era of transportation. In the early 1900s, gasoline-powered automobiles quickly became a popular form of transportation. By 1916

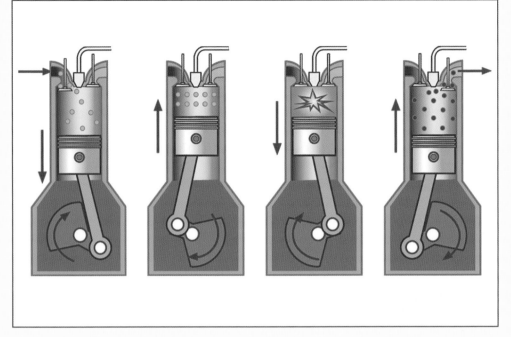

Combustion Engine

In a combustion engine, fuel is inserted into a cylinder called a piston. The fuel gets compressed and lit, creating a small explosion. The explosion pushes the piston down so that it can be refilled with fuel. The up and down energy of the pistons gets converted into rotating energy in the crankshaft. The spinning crankshaft powers the wheels on the vehicle. Can you identify the crankshaft in the diagram above?

tanks were introduced into World War I. Tanks were fitted with caterpillar tracks, which are plated bands that go around the wheels. These wide tracks have a large surface area. They spread out the tank's weight. This allows tanks to travel over muddy land without sinking.

A tank's body must be strong enough to protect it from bullets and missiles. But it must also be light enough to allow the tank to move easily. Modern tanks are made of layers of steel with other materials sandwiched in. Together these materials resist impacts and absorb heat from missiles and other weapons.

War on Water

Traveling by ship gives warriors the opportunity to fight in faraway lands. Ships also allow countries to patrol and protect their coastlines. All seaworthy ships must be buoyant and have a reliable power source.

When a ship is placed on water, it displaces, or pushes aside, a certain amount of water. At the same time, the water pushes on the ship with an upward force. This is the buoyant force. An object's buoyancy depends on its density. Objects that are less dense than water float. The size of the object does not matter.

From 800 to 1100 CE, Viking warriors ruled the seas of northern Europe. Viking craftsmen used their

Longships were also called dragonships because of their decorative carvings.

expertise to create warships. They were known as longships because of their long, narrow design. The shape helped longships displace less water than wider ships did. Longships rode high in the water. Like most ships, the longship had a piece of wood that ran along its bottom. This piece is called a keel. Keels help keep boats upright in waves. But unlike most ocean-going boats, longboats had very shallow keels. This allowed the boats to travel up rivers and over sandbars. Viking warriors could come ashore almost anywhere.

Longships used large square sails to harness wind power. The force of wind blowing on the sail propelled the ship forward. Longships were also fitted with up to 72 oars. Warriors could use muscle power to move the ship quickly.

In 1815 the first steam-powered warship was built for the US Navy. Steamships would go on

Submarines

Like ships, submarines rely on the force of buoyancy. But submarines can control their buoyancy. They use tanks that can be filled with water or air. The crew controls the submarine's density by filling the tanks with air. Air-filled tanks make the submarine less dense, making it float. When it is time to dive, the tanks get filled with water. The submarine becomes denser and dives. When the submarine needs to surface, the water is pushed out and the tanks are filled with air.

Aircraft carriers allow navies to spread out their air forces around the world.

to replace most sailing ships in battle. Steam ships used steam engines powered by coal. Burning coal heats water in a boiler, creating steam. The steam travels into a cylinder where it pushes a piston. The piston is attached to the propellers. As the piston moves back and forth, it drives the propellers, moving the ship forward.

Today many navies include massive aircraft carriers. An aircraft carrier is a warship with a flight deck. Warplanes can take off and land on the carrier's runway. Aircraft carriers are floating cities more than 1,000 feet (305 m) long. Aircraft carriers are powered by nuclear reactors. A nuclear reactor produces heat by splitting atoms. The heat then turns water into steam. The steam is controlled and channeled. It creates a force that turns turbine engines that, in turn, power the carrier's propellers.

Armed in the Air

World War I was the first time that soldiers took to the air to fight. Early fighter planes were made from wood. They had two sets of wings and engines that powered propellers. The plane's propeller gives it thrust. Thrust helps planes overcome the force of drag caused by the air around it as well as friction from the tires touching the ground. As a plane moves forward, air passes over its wings. The wings have a special shape, called an airfoil. They are curved on top and flat underneath. Air moves faster over the top of the wings. This creates lower air pressure above the wings. The difference in pressure over and under the wings causes the plane to rise.

Over the years, there have been many advancements in airplane technology. Planes are now controlled with computers and electronics. In the newest control systems, pilots put commands into a computer. The computers automatically adjust parts of the plane, such as the wing flaps or tail. This makes flights safer and more stable.

Beyond Warfare

The science of warfare has always driven changes in technology that have made wars increasingly devastating. But the same advancements that have given nations the edge in warfare have also created benefits in other fields such as medicine, transportation, and communication. Understanding science has made these achievements possible.

In September 1916, the tank was first used on the battlefield. A 19-year-old soldier named Bert Chaney described seeing a tank for the first time:

> We heard strange throbbing noises, and lumbering slowly towards us came three huge mechanical monsters such as we had never seen before. My first impression was that they looked ready to topple on their noses, but their tails and the two little wheels at the back held them down and kept them level. Big metal things they were, with two sets of caterpillar wheels that went right round the body. There was a huge bulge on each side with a door in the bulging part, and machine guns on swivels poked out from either side. The engine, a petrol engine of massive proportions, occupied practically all the inside space. Mounted behind each door was a motorcycle type of saddle seat and there was just enough room left for the belts of ammunition and the drivers.
>
> Source: "The Battlefield Debut of the Tank, 1916." Eyewitness to History. Ibis Communications Inc., 2005. Web. Accessed February 29, 2016.

What's the Big Idea?

Read the passage carefully. What is the main idea? How does the soldier react to seeing a tank? What details support this idea? Write down the details and describe how they support the main idea.

FAST FACTS

- Warfare sometimes brings about major advancements in technology.
- Clubs use mass and speed to gain more momentum and cause greater damage.
- Copper was the first metal used to make swords.
- Tin was added to copper to create bronze, which made longer, harder weapons.
- In approximately 1200 BCE, metalworkers started using iron and steel, which could be forged into even longer and harder weapons.
- All projectiles must overcome the forces of drag and gravity in order to be effective.
- Cannons and guns use chemical reactions to power projectiles.
- Some missiles use radar, which works by sending out signals and waiting for them to return.
- Chain mail was designed to protect against slashing swords, but advancements in bow technology made people begin to use plate armor.

- Camouflage works by breaking up a person's outline, making it unrecognizable to human eyes.
- The steam engine, internal combustion engine, and nuclear engine each changed how militaries moved.
- Submarines are able to change their buoyancy in order to rise or sink.
- Airplanes use airfoils to create pressure differences that cause the planes to rise.

STOP AND THINK

Tell the Tale

Chapter Three discusses how science helped improve body armor. Imagine you are a soldier getting ready for battle. Write 200 words describing who you are and how you will protect your body with armor. What will you wear on your head? What armor will you use to cover the rest of your body? What is the armor made of?

Take a Stand

Science and technology have been used in warfare for centuries. Some advancements, such as armor, save lives. Others, such as bombs, are meant to kill. Are there benefits to scientific development for military purposes? Do you think that science and technology should be used for war? Why or why not?

Surprise Me

Chapter Four describes the science behind military vehicles. After reading this chapter, what two or three facts about how military vehicles work did you find most surprising? Write a few sentences about each fact. Why did you find each fact surprising?

You Are There

This book discusses the invention of Kevlar. Imagine you are a scientist working in a laboratory. You are working on a product that will help soldiers. Write a letter home telling your friends about your new invention. What is your invention? How will your invention be used by soldiers?

GLOSSARY

alloy
a metal made by melting and mixing two or more metals

axle
a rod around which a wheel turns

combustion
a chemical reaction that produces heat and light

forge
to form something by heating and shaping metal

friction
the force between two surfaces that resists motion

medieval
having to do with the Middle Ages

mimic
to imitate something else

missile
a weapon that is shot through the sky over a distance and then falls to the ground and explodes

payload
the mass of material delivered by a weapon

piston
a short cylinder that moves up and down against a liquid or gas in a tube

projectile
something thrown or launched through the air

trajectory
the curved path along which something moves through the air or through space

LEARN MORE

Books

Allen, John. *High-Tech Weapons*. San Diego, CA: Blackbirch, 2005.

Perritano, John, and James Spears. *Everything Battles*. Washington, DC: National Geographic, 2013.

Websites

To learn more about Super-Awesome Science, visit **booklinks.abdopublishing.com**. These links are routinely monitored and updated to provide the most current information available.

Visit **mycorelibrary.com** for free additional tools for teachers and students.

INDEX

ABOUT THE AUTHOR

Cecilia Pinto McCarthy has written several nonfiction books for children. She also teaches environmental science classes at a nature sanctuary. She and her family live north of Boston, Massachusetts.